P9-ECW-686

Wannabe Guide to
GOLF

by

JACK MINGO

RDR Books
Oakland, California

RDR Books
4456 Piedmont
Oakland, CA 94611

Copyright 1997 by Jack Mingo

ISBN 1-57143-040-7
Library of Congress Card Catalog Number 97-066926

Cover image and design: Bonnie Smetts Design
Book Design: Richard Harris / Paula Morrison
Illustrations: Sergei Ponomarov
Editing: Bob Drews
Production: Jesse McKinney, Lee Broat

Printed in the United States of America
by Thomson-Shore, Inc.

Distributed in Canada by Orca Book Co., Victoria, BC

Distributed in Great Britain and Europe by Airlift Book
Company, Enfield, Middlesex, United Kingdom

Contents

Why Learn About Golf?

In the words of long-time pro Greg Norman, "Golf is like a cat chasing its tail. You're never going to catch it. The day you think you've got your game down pat, something goes awry and you're back to square one. That's one reason why I love the game so much: the soul-searching and the never-ending search for the perfect swing."

For many, golf is a game, a pastime, a diversion. For many others, millions of others, golf is a passion, an addiction, a pursuit that can make obligations to family and career secondary. Of course, that only happens to the other person. You, no doubt, will be able to golf sensibly and not get hooked, to back away any time you want.

Sure.

How popular is golf? According to the National Golf Foundation, there are more than 18 million golfers in the United States. (And on some weekends, it will seem as if all 18 million are on the course ahead of you.) Heaven only knows how many more legions will be added in the enthusiasm over the young sensation, Tiger Woods.

Golf, understandably, is a big business. Around the country there are about 13,000 golf courses and practice facilities. The National Sporting Goods Association reports that golfers spend about $600 million every year on equipment—clubs, carts, shoes and golf balls to replace those wayward shots that landed in the water, the rough or some poor soul's windshield.

Why is golf so successful ?

Aside from its charms and challenges, golf at its essence is very easy and very difficult. Game designers have a truism that the best game is one simple enough that new players can begin playing it in minutes . . . but difficult enough that they can spend the rest of their lives trying to master it.

Golf has delightful oddities:

- The lower your score, the better you're doing.
- The ball has dimples.
- The weird-looking clubs have odd names and numbers. Actually, once upon a time they had even weirder names like "mashie" and "niblick," which now just sound like they should be brand names belonging to the Green Giant company.

Like any group of aficionados and fanatics, golfers have their own language, traditions, habits, laws, legends, myths, superstitions and ways of dealing with "outsiders." In this book we will introduce you to them and give you a feel for the game, its maddening difficulties, its delightful quirks, its sweet sensations such as learning how to plop the ball onto the green from 100 yards away on a delightful spring morning with the smell of freshly cut grass in the air.

What this book cannot do is make you into a good golfer. We will tell you the basics, and then it is up to you to learn them, work on them and develop them to whatever level of skill you can achieve. But just remember: Anybody who has ever watched a golf tournament knows that this is a game that can cause even a professional golfer with decades of experience to self-destruct on any given afternoon. Get your hopes high as you undertake the golf adventure but don't let a little white ball cause you to go ballistic.

Whether you are already one of the initiated 18 million or a wannabe member of this ever-growing club, let this book ease you out of the roughs and bunkers of life and land you on the smooth, grassy greens of the game of golf.

The Object of the Game

Who doesn't know the object of a golf game? ("To win, of course," says a voice from the back.)

The object of golf is this: Using your collection of clubs you try to hit the ball from point A, the tee, to point B (sometimes known as "point %$#&*!"), that little hole over there with the flag sticking out (called "the hole" or "the cup"). You try to do so in the fewest number of strokes, all of which are counted (whether you actually connect with the ball or not).

That sounds easy enough, and it is—in theory. Which is why golf course designers make things interesting (for them, at least). Going from point A to point B is never the same from hole to hole and course to course. Sometimes a hole is in a straight direction. Sometimes it is curved. Sometimes it doubles back on itself. The distance from the tee to the cup can vary widely, anywhere from 85 to 600 yards (and even more in some cases). As if that weren't enough, there are obstacles along the way—water, trees, sand traps (sometimes called "bunkers"). Designing courses requires a knowledge of landscape and a genuine streak of sadism; a designer is not only a Duke of Landscaping, but a Marquis de Sod.

So, the idea is to hit the ball smoothly from the tee, up the main stretch of grass called the "fairway," onto the very smooth patch of grass called the "green" and into the hole, all the while never hitting the ball too far or not far enough; avoiding sand, water, trees, never losing your ball or your temper, and generally saying to yourself, "This is only a game."

See how easy this is?

The Game

The idea of golf is to get the ball into the hole with as few strokes as possible.

The standard golf course is 18 holes. This is a completely arbitrary number based on the number of holes that fit into the Old Course at St. Andrews in Scotland. There are nine-hole courses, as well. "Hole" is confusing, because it not only is used to mean the cup you're shooting at but also the whole field of play that leads up to the cup, from the tee to the far end of the green. So the "18th hole" refers to the entire expanse of grass, sand, woods, ponds and any of the other inanimate objects you might hit along the way. (The "19th hole," of course, is the bar.)

Each hole has a rating called "par," defined as the score an expert would be expected to score on a fair to good day if sober. Par is determined by such factors as length, terrain and hazards. The truly good golfer consistently achieves par or even below par, which for some golfers is a problem because they become confused and also strive to be below par in work, family life and friendships.

For efficiency, safety and to make sure golfers are not unduly subjected to dangerous fresh air, heart-rending exercise or carcinogenic sunlight, courses are nearly always laid out in a series of loops, so that the next hole begins where the last one ended. You're supposed to play them in order—in fact, you will be disqualified if you're caught going out of sequence during a tournament. (There are reports that during the Elvis Presley Invitational in Memphis, you can also be disqualified for playing out of sequins, but that's a whole 'nother story, Thankyewverymuch!)

Here's another confusing thing: the tee. It also refers to two things. One of them is the little wooden thing that you stick in the ground and hit your ball from at the beginning of each hole. Tees also make halfway decent ad-hoc toothpicks, if you wipe the dirt off first. You can understand why they're called "tees," because they're sort of T-shaped, if you squint and use your imagination.

Wooden tees are a fairly recent invention (Before that, they used little piles of wet sand to hold the ball off the ground.), and they get their name from the second thing called a "tee" in golf: the area from which you first hit your ball (officially referred to as the "teeing ground"). Before this was called a "tee" it was a "teez" in 17th-century Scotland. Nobody quite knows what "teez" meant on those early Scottish golf courses, but the name's been handed down to us, and I guess we're stuck with it.

The teeing ground usually has three sets of markers. Sometimes these are sensible little metal signs, but course designers often feel compelled to get cute with these, so watch it. They might be giant pop-art golf balls, or driftwood, or rocks, or even little statues of mermaids, trolls or the Unknown Golfer. The point of the markers is to define the areas where it's legal to tee off from; they're set up so that people can play the same hole from a variety of lengths. Usually, they're color-coded: The red area, closest to the green, is considered the so-called "ladies' course." The white markers in the middle define the "duffer's course" and is played by the great majority of players. Finally, the blue markers way in the back indicate the official championship course, used only by professionals, talented amateurs and optimistic overachievers.

So let's say you've got all the gear and are ready to become a golfer. Where do you begin? On the first hole, of course. Show up at your pre-arranged tee time and when it's your turn, select the right club (see page 31) and step up to the tee. Jam your tee in the ground behind the red, white or blue markers and place your ball on top of it.

Address the ball. (This is not saying, "Hello, ball." Rather you are getting into the proper stance and preparing to hit the ball with that big club called the "driver.") But first look up. If the clubhouse is looming in front of you, STOP AND TURN AROUND! You should be looking at the flag of the first hole looming in the distance. Figure out where you want to hit the ball, say a prayer, and let 'er rip.

That's a "stroke." Count it for your scorecard. Each time you swing at the ball, even if you miss or send it soaring only six inches, it counts as a stroke. You also get strokes counted for various penalties. But more about that later.

After all of the players in your group have teed-off, the next turn goes to the person who's "away" (meaning the one with the ball farthest from the cup), so let's hope you watched where your ball went. It might have landed on the green a few feet from the tee, if you believe in golf fairies, but more likely it ended up on the fairway, in the rough or into a hazard.

The fairway is the smooth turf between the tee and the green. The rough can be any number of things, none of them good news: snake-infested weeds, thorny thickets, long grass, trees, bushes or paths. And hazards can be enough to make grown golfers weep, moan, tear their plaids and promise to give up the game and live a life of virtue.

The Game

Hazards come in two flavors: bunkers and water. Bunkers are filled with what the foolish man builds his house upon—sand. Sometimes called "sand traps," bunkers can be as level as a sandbox or a deep hole that you have to crawl into. Water, of course, includes everything you think it would, and a few you might not think of: lakes, ponds, streams, ditches, lagoons, rivers, oceans, swamps, even large, deep puddles from heavy rainstorms.

Bad as bunkers are, they can be played out of, at least in theory, with enough blasting and swearing. If the water is just a puddle, you can try hitting the ball out. But with most water hazards, however, even swearing won't usually help. Give it up, fish your ball out of the alligator-infested swamp, take a one-stroke penalty and play your ball from a point along the path of your previous shot.

At least the penalty makes sense. Less logical is the one-stroke penalty for "grounding your club" (touching the ground with it) when your ball's in a hazard of any kind. You can also get a one-stroke penalty in formal play for either advising or asking for advice from anyone other than your caddie (the person who hauls around your clubs so you are free to think about why you dubbed that last shot) or your partner, which sounds ludicrous at first but will make all the sense in the world once you've ever played with an annoying know-it-all. For more rules, see page 84.

When you find your ball and it's your turn to go again, remember that you must play the ball "as she lays." That means you can't—with very few exceptions (see Rules)—pick it up, move it or even touch it. Furthermore, you have to play the course as you find it. You can't move, bend, break or press anything down to improve your swing, your ball's position or the ball's expected path of travel.

As you swing at the ball (perhaps again and again and again) remember that your immediate goal is to get on the green near the hole. If you're "away" you keep hitting until you get closer to the hole than somebody else—then that person is "away" and hits until they are no longer farthest.

Once you hit the green and are getting ready to use that short club with the flat head known as "the putter," you might find that your ball is in the way of somebody else's. Such a situation used to be considered one of the hazards of the game. However, after a couple of crucial tournaments were decided by players hitting their opponent's ball afield as if playing croquet, the rules were changed in the 1950s. Now it's considered good form (not to mention smart) to press a marker into the ground and remove your ball if there's any chance somebody's shot might come close to it.

Finally, holding the flag if others are getting close enough to get their ball into the cup is considered good form, as is reporting an accurate count of your strokes and penalties.

Putting in Time: The Origins of Golf

Who invented golf? Ha! You might as well ask another imponderable, like which is the one true religion, or whether Coke is better than Pepsi.

The answer depends on whom you ask, what nationality you are, how desperately you want to believe your own pet theory, and what you mean by "golf." The idea of taking a stick and hitting something spherical into a hole in the ground is such a no-brain invention that evidence seems to indicate that the basic game was invented time and again throughout history—perhaps prehistory, even, if you're willing to accept that old *Flintstones* reruns make pretty credible documentation.

We do know that the early Romans played a hole-in-the-ground game called *"paganica."* (We don't know if the pagans returned the favor by playing a game called "romanica.") It was played with a bent stick and a leather ball filled with feathers. (See page 51 for more information on how those early golf balls were direct descendants.)

We also know that modern-day golf has been around since before Columbus got over the water hazard we call the Atlantic Ocean. An act of Parliament dated March 6, 1457, refers to a decree by James II of Scotland, in which he banned both golf and "football" because their popularity was interfering with archery practice, reducing his army's readiness to do battle against the soldiers of England. (After a peace treaty was signed in 1503, the ban was rescinded except "in tyme of sermonis" on Sundays.) But beyond this, the theories are as varied as the golf swing.

Scotland

The traditional theory, first put forth by Sir W. G. Simpson in his 1887 book, *The Art of Golf,* is still favored by most golfers and virtually all Scots. Simpson's guess was that golf was invented by shepherds tending their flocks by night outside the town of St. Andrews, Scotland. He hypothesized that some bored shepherd, looking for diversion, idly hit at a small stone with his staff. By crook and then by hook, the stone curved slightly, landed and rolled right into a rabbit hole, for the first hole in one. Another shepherd saw this and challenged him to do it again, and the first golf game began. (Another theory, also without any documented evidence whatsoever, is that *paganica* might have been left behind in Scotland by the Romans centuries earlier.)

Holland

The *Rothmans Atlas of World Sport* says the game is believed to have derived either from a British stick-and-ball game known as "knur and spell" or the Dutch game *kolven. Kolven* is an especially strong contender. It was played on any surface available, including ice. The only problem with this theory is that while there are many paintings of Dutch people playing *kolven,* the earliest known documentation doesn't go back any farther than the early 1600s. Still, *kolven* makes a historical mark as the earliest documented golf-like game in America: Historians have found a warrant sworn out against three Dutch immigrants in 1651 for playing *kolven* on a day of public prayer.

Putting in Time: The Origins of Golf

Belgium
References to Belgium's *chole* go back to the 1300s. It was played sort of like golf, but both sides played the same ball. (That only happens occasionally now, and usually by accident.)

France
Some people, most of whom are French, believe that the ancient French game *jeu de mail* bears the closest resemblance to modern golf. The game was played on open land with the first stroke hit from a tee and subsequent strokes played from where the ball landed. Whoever reached a predetermined point in the least number of strokes won.

China
Not to be confused with Polo, as in Marco, golf might have come from China. According to a Chinese historian named Ling Hong-ling, 10th-century Chinese pottery and paintings depict a game very much like modern golf, five centuries before the Scots' earliest documentation. The game, first mentioned in a document in 943 A.D., was called *"chuiwan,"* meaning "hitting ball." Hong-ling believes that early travelers brought the game to Europe in the Middle Ages, where it evolved a little further into what we called "golf." The popularity of *chuiwan* eventually died out in China in the 1500s, a few decades after golf was "invented" in Scotland.

The St. Andrews Golf Course

Regardless of whoever truly invented golf, the prototype of the modern golf course is found in Scotland, at a pilgrimage site for duffers worldwide called the "Old Course" at St. Andrews. Situated on 93½ acres of grass-covered sand dunes linking the town and the Bay of St. Andrews, the course was christened by an archbishop on January 25, 1552, who sanctioned the use of the "linksland" for the local community to rear rabbits and "play at golf, futball, and schute-ing." This was the origin of the use of "links" to refer to a golf course. Other tidbits of trivia:

• An account has it that the course used to have 19 holes, but that one hole was removed to lengthen the others. The 18-hole model became a prototype for the other courses of the world.

• For hundreds of years, the only grass cutting was done by sheep and rabbits. To this day, the course has no trees, which is both a blessing (fewer obstacles) and a curse (nothing to block the formidable wind).

• Although there are 18 holes, there are only 11 greens. The first, ninth, 17th and 18th holes have their own greens—the rest share with another, their numbers always adding up to 18 (the second hole with the 16th, the third with the 15th, etc.)

• The course wasn't designed by a person, but by God, say the people of St. Andrews, a result of Nature with minimal

improvements. For example, St. Andrews' sand traps were created when grazing sheep burrowed into the sand dunes to escape the heavy wind off the ocean. Golf course designers around the world have gone to great lengths to duplicate the course's naturally-occurring doglegs, hazards and sand-filled bunker holes.

• The sand traps are steep and deep, more difficult than most. There are lots of "pothole bunkers" just big enough for one cursing golfer and a golf club (or one windblown sheep). Some of them are so notorious they have been given (not just called) names, including the Coffins, Principal's Nose, Beardies, Elysian Fields and Hell.

• The Old Course is only one of five at St. Andrews. There are also the "New" Course (built in 1895), the Jubilee (1897), the Eden (1914) and the Strathtyrum (1993).

Scoring

"Golf is a game in which you yell 'fore,' shoot six and write down five."
—Paul Harvey

Scoring golf is pretty easy, yet you'd be amazed at the number of people—even accountants and mathematicians—who suddenly have trouble remembering how to count when they're whacking at a ball in the middle of a field.

The score you get for each hole is the number of "strokes" you take to get the ball from the tee and into the cup. The rules say that you count one stroke any time you swing at the ball. Practice strokes don't count unless you accidentally hit your ball. Making sure you're standing well away from the ball when you practice will ensure that nobody will think you're trying to hit your ball . . . and that you don't accidentally do so.

Besides actual strokes, there are penalties that count as extra strokes. The penalties differ depending on whether you're playing a match or stroke game; and there are esoteric exceptions, so you might want to pick up a Professional Golfers Association rule book that you can read and tuck into your bag.

Here are some examples of penalties: Playing the wrong ball or moving a ball, either accidentally or on purpose. You'll get a penalty if you lose your ball and can't find it, or if you know where your ball is, can't play it and have to move it into a playable position. If you hit your partner, it will cost you two strokes. (But, strangely, you incur no penalty for hitting an opponent.) Two strokes is also the penalty if your ball hits another ball on the green. (But not the fairway. There, you play it where it lies and the other ball gets replaced in its original spot.) You can even get penalties for acts of God: After you address your ball, if it moves for any reason before you hit it, you take a penalty stroke (a reason to not dawdle when playing in wind or in seismically active locations like California and Hawaii).

Of course, some players seem inclined to give themselves whatever score they think they deserve for each hole . . . so if they feel they've received an unfair penalty, they find a way to make it up in their score somewhere else.

Par

"We're playing a game where the aim is to be below par. It's so wrong for me!"

—Stephanie Vanderkeller, *Newhart*

As I said before, each hole is assigned a score called "par," which is supposed to indicate what the best golfers would score on a fair to good day. But how courses assign par to each hole is intriguing. Rather than getting professionals to come and play, the courses rely on the United States Golfing Association, which has issued elaborate guidelines on how to determine what it is.

Par is to be three, four, five or six strokes. Generally, a par three hole measures less than 250 yards (210 for women) from tee to cup; a par four hole, between 251 and 470 yards (211 to 400 for women); a par five hole, 471 to 690 yards (401 to 590 for women); and the rare par six hole 691 yards or more (591 for women).

The par rating is based on the assumption that a first-rate golfer will take two strokes *on* the green; the additional strokes are what he or she will take getting *to* the green. However, the yardage rules above are just rules of thumb. The "configuration of the ground and the severity of the obstacles" also figure into it, to quote the USGA.

Par for each hole appears on your scorecard. Next to it is a place for your actual score. Prepare for some discrepancy between the two—most likely yours will usually be on the high side. But not always. Sometimes you'll make par on a hole, and even beat it.

What's it called if you beat par? Not "a miracle!" Instead, the jargon is heavy on our feathered friends, for some reason. If you take one stroke less than par, it's called a "birdie." If two strokes, it's an "eagle." If three strokes, it's called a "double eagle."

On the more likely side of par, one stroke over par is called a "bogey," two strokes, a "double bogey," three strokes, a "triple bogey," and so on. The reason it's called a bogey is not after Humphrey Bogart, even though that was his nickname. It's probably from the meaning of the word as used in "bogeyman," meaning a hobgoblin or Satan himself. "Colonel Bogey's March" is a well-known British military tune; as a result, in England, "Colonel Bogey" is a name given to represent the imaginary average player—golfers there talk about "beating bogey" or "beating the colonel" if they score par or below. (Oddly, "Under the Double Eagle" is a famous American march. Does this mean American march composers were really that much better golfers than the British?)

Handicap

"What's your handicap?" asks the duffer's partner as they

prepare to tee off. He thinks for a moment before answering earnestly. "Well, putting and driving mostly."

In such games as tennis, chess, darts and corporate one-upsmanship, the stronger or smarter player will nearly always beat the weaker player. But remember how we said earlier that golf has a style of its own? Welcome to the delightful quirk of handicapping. Perhaps to avoid the tortuous tedium of having your ego destroyed in slow motion on a sunny afternoon by a player in a different league than yours—or perhaps to avoid the unpleasant scene of fist-fights on a tranquil green—the system of handicapping came into popularity. It's slightly similar in some ways to the point spread in gambling, where it's possible for a team to lose a game, but for betting purposes "win" if it does better than expected. Handicapping assesses your abilities (or lack thereof) and assigns you a number of points that make up for your weaknesses as a player. The idea is to give all players, no matter how good or bad, an equal chance of winning a game.

Your handicap is figured by looking at your scores over time and figuring out how many strokes it would take to reduce your score to par. For example, if your scores have been typically 94 on a par 72 course, your handicap would be 22. If you belong to a golf club, they will traditionally do the math for you, using USGA formulas.

Once you have that number, what do you do with it? Well, in formal competition, you turn in your scorecard with two scores on it, the gross score (your actual strokes) and the net score (strokes with handicap subtracted). Let's say you claim a 112 for a gross score—subtracting your handicap of 22 gives you a net score of 90.

In a "match-play" game against another player, it's a little more complicated. If you've got a handicap of 22 and your opponent has a handicap of 19, you take the difference—three—and look at your scorecard for the three most difficult holes—the ones with the highest par. You subtract one stroke from each of them when you add up your final score.

Your handicap is recalibrated periodically, so you're actually playing against your average self in every game to see if you do better or worse than normal.

Stroke or Match Play?

"Stroke play is a better test of golf, but match play is a better test of character."   —Joe Carr

There are two ways to play golf—stroke and match. Stroke play is the form you see on television, in which the number of strokes is totaled during the game and whoever has the least for the whole game wins. Match play is much more common among amateurs. In this case, you compete for each individual hole. You (or you and your partner in a foursome) win by having the lowest score in the greatest number of holes. As a result, it isn't at all uncommon for a golfer to have the highest total number of strokes but still win the game because he or she won 10 or more holes. It's sort of like the Electoral College in American presidential races.

The Fundamentals

"No one who ever had lessons would have a swing like mine."
                                    —Lee Trevino

The theory behind golf is easy enough. You take the clubs, hit the ball around the course, aim for a little hole, and then you get mad and throw your clubs into the water hazard, vowing to never play again. But as we all know, theory and practice can be two entirely different things.

Basic to moving from theory to practice is developing proper fundamentals that carry you from tee to green and away from roughs and hazards that can turn a pleasant morning or afternoon into an agonizing exercise.

The Grip

There's an old saying: "Old golfers never die, they just lose their grip." How you hold the club is so important that experts recommend that beginners consult with a professional instructor. "If you can afford only one lesson," says one, "spend it learning how to grip the club and how to swing back." (Of course, if you can afford only one lesson, what are you doing taking up golf in the first place?)

Your grip does two things: It aims the club face in the direction you hope to hit the ball, and it translates the power of your swing from your body and arms into your golf club.

Here are the fundamentals of grip for a right-hander. If you're left-handed, reverse all directions (except, of course, directions like forward, backward, up and down). Let's see how well you follow complicated instructions. (Have a golf pro check your grip once you think you've got it down.)

1. Pick a club, any club at all, and place the club head end on the ground. Point the club's face (the hitting side) toward your target, and the shaft of the club in your hand tilting slightly toward your target. Now figure out which is your left hand, because we're going to get it positioned first.

2. LEFT HAND. Hold your left hand loosely with the palm up. Take that tilting club shaft and, a few inches from the top, lean it across your open palm. Wrap your fingers around the handle grip with your left thumb pointing straight down the shaft just to the right of the center of the handle as you look down at it. Keep your thumb and forefinger fairly loose, and hold your club mostly with the last three fingers of your left hand. If you're doing it right, the "V" of your thumb and forefinger is pointing toward your right shoulder.

3. RIGHT HAND: This is called the "overlap grip," and this is why: Take your right hand and place it firmly against the shaft just below your left hand. Curl your fingers around the grip. Now here comes the weird part, which separates playing golf from batting a baseball. Slide your right hand up and rest your right little finger between your left forefinger and middle finger (known as the "bird" in freeway driving jargon). Position your right finger left of the center line of your shaft. Hold the club lightly between your right thumb and the crook of your right forefinger "as if holding a butterfly," to quote one expert.

Why the overlap grip? It doesn't feel natural, and it isn't. Why not just hold the club like an axe and whack away at the ball? For the same reason Lizzie Borden and Paul Bunyan weren't known for their golf games. Like a number of skills

you'll learn from the game, a good golf grip is pretty much good for nothing but golf.

Addressing the Ball

Many beginners hear the phrase "addressing the ball" and wonder about it. Or as one confused soul put it, "I can see why you'd want to put your name on your ball in case you lose it, but what if you break someone's windshield or something? If you have your address on your ball, they know where to come and get you."

Despite what you might have seen on reruns of the old Jackie Gleason comedy show, *The Honeymooners,* addressing the ball is not like Ed Norton tipping his hat and saying "Hello, ball." While it is true that most golfers do talk to the ball at some time or other—everything from "Ball, you will go straight and true," intoned by New Age inner-game acolytes to "You %$#@&#ing ball!" from everybody else—"addressing the ball" simply means positioning yourself as you prepare to hit it.

Aim

Now that you've put your hands where they belong, let's get the rest of your body to do its stuff. Once you've gotten your hands around the right club for the shot (Clubs are discussed on pages 31-39.), you need to align your body in such a way that there's a chance the ball will actually go where you want it to go.

Your first step is figuring out the shot. Stand behind the ball and look toward your target. That can be the flag of the hole, or on a curving "dogleg" hole, it could be a point midway through the curve to set up your next shot. Of course, if there are heavy cross winds or a slope you may want to allow for that by aiming upwind or uphill.

When they've lined up the shot, many golfers look for a "siter,"—a twig or other small landmark on the ground that's along your line but a few feet ahead of the ball. The idea is to have something you can line up with when you look down and address your ball. This is not to be confused with a "sitar," which is what Ravi Shankar probably would have used if he had taught Beatle George Harrison how to line up shots.

Stance

Take your club and place its "face" (the hitting side) behind the ball. Keeping your club in this position, place your feet. Your distance from the ball will depend on the length of the club and what feels comfortable when you keep its head level.

When preparing to drive the ball (hitting it hard off the

tee), position your feet so the ball is lined up to a spot just inside your left heel. When you're lucky enough to have reached a position to putt, your left heel should be four to six inches ahead of the ball. A line drawn across both your feet would not only make a dandy golf fashion statement, but should, most experts say, be exactly parallel to the line that you hope your ball will travel. (Some experts suggest an "open" stance in which you aren't quite parallel but face slightly toward the target. Facing slightly away from the target is called a "closed" stance. It's usually not recommended because it makes it harder to see where your ball's going to go.) If driving, your feet span should be about six inches wider than your shoulders; if putting, it should be no wider than your shoulders; and if you're using a wedge to get out of a sand trap, it should be about half-shoulder width.

The weight of your body should be directly behind the balls of your feet. Bend your body forward slightly, but hold your head aligned straight with your spine and behind the ball, so you can actually see the part of the ball you're going to hit when you swing. Now, put your club head up to the ball, and relax your knees and your arms. You might try breathing a quick silent prayer. (Don't laugh, a poll found that, whether religious or not, 75% of all professional golfers admit to praying during games. Apparently there are few atheists in fairways and bunkers—something ministers and priests should remember before complaining about people playing golf on Sunday mornings instead of coming to church.)

The Swing

"It don't mean a thing if it ain't got that swing . . ."
—Duke Ellington

The Duke's right. All the preparation of grip and stance is just prelude—"fore" play, as it were—to the main event of hitting your ball a country mile off the tee (and then getting it to the green from the fairway in subsequent shots, known as "approach shots"). If your swing off the tee is lousy, you'll be lucky to hit it a country furlong, and it will go anyplace other than where you intend.

Here's a secret to a good swing: a certain fluidity of body motion. "If you can dance, you can easily learn a good swing," says one expert, observing that the entire body—not just the arms—gets involved in the movement. So, if your dancing isn't up to par, your golf score may never get down to par.

But wait. Before changing into tights and a ballet outfit (which would be just tu-tu much), let's see if we can help you get in the dancing mood with just some good instructions, literally from the ground up.

One Good Turn Deserves Another
Let's start with the feet. Your feet shouldn't move from their firmly planted position when you swing. That means everything else has to, turning around from the ankles to the shoulders.

The Swing

Shifting your weight is crucial. Try a practice swing and see how your weight shifts on your feet as you do it. You (if right-handed) start with your weight more on your left heel, and when you swing back shift your weight to your right heel (not the outside of your foot), and almost completely off your left foot. As you bring the club forward, your weight should then shift again from your right heel to your left. At your follow-through after you hit the ball, your right foot should be almost completely off the ground, with only your big toe still touching planet Earth.

Many golfers have trouble bringing their whole body into the swing, and resist the shifting of weight, fearing they'll lose their balance if they don't keep their bodies as upright and rigid as possible. Actually, though, the weight shift is what gives you a lot of the power in your swing and regulates its tempo. Even though he was a physicist, Isaac (Izzy) Newton could've been a golf pro when he came up with the tip that a body moving has more momentum than one at rest.

One problem with this twist is that some golfers don't go far enough with it. Others go too far and actually tilt. Tilting can ruin your game in pinball, and it can do the same in golf. Your shoulders should stay relatively level with the ground or you won't get the right weight shift.

One strange thing that happens in a good swing is that your club rotates a full half-turn. Not that your club moves inside your grip, but that it naturally rolls in the air with the movement of your wrists and body. In fact, the best way to screw up your natural swing is to try to figure out how to keep your club face facing in the right direction throughout it. Think of it, and try it with your swing: The club face starts square at the ball. As you swing back, watch the "toe" of the club head. (Hey, if that's the club's "head," shouldn't the toe be called the "nose"?) When the club in your back swing is hip-high and parallel with the ground, the toe of your club is pointing straight up in the air. When you swing forward, watch your club in the same position in follow-through—again, the toe is (or should be) pointing straight up. So if someone tells you that your swing has gone "completely toes up" it might be a compliment. Or maybe not.

To Go Forward, You Must Go Back

The back swing should move fluidly and naturally, using your left hand and arm (if right-handed) to push the club straight back from the ball. At the top of the swing, your club should be just about exactly horizontal behind your head and pointing toward the spot you're aiming at. (How you're supposed to tell whether you're doing that while keeping your head down is anybody's guess.)

While your club goes up, your hips should stay still until the movement of your shoulder muscles pulls them around as you approach the top of your back swing. You want your hips to remain as still as possible for as long as possible, because you're coiling your muscles from shoulders to hips like a tightly wound watch mainspring. (Do watches even have mainsprings any more? I guess not. There goes a really good metaphor, sacrificed on the altar of modern technology. How about a more up-to-date one? "You're coiling your muscles from shoulders to hips like flicking the lash of a buggy whip"—there we go, much better.)

As your club goes up and over, your shoulders rotate around your head, as if you were trying out for a part in *The Exorcist*. Your left shoulder ends up directly in front of your face, your right shoulder directly behind your head. The tendency for some new golfers is to let the shoulder in front drop, but this is a fatal error. (Well, not fatal to you as a human being, just to your golf game, RIP.) Neither shoulder should tilt up or down, because it's this smooth pivot that'll give you all your power. If you do it right, you'll feel your body weight shift naturally to your right foot as if you're dancing the two-step; if you do it wrong, you'll feel something weighing as heavily on your left hip as a bad conscience.

With a Swing and a Prayer

As you hit the top of your back swing, don't hesitate. Despite seeing still photos of people frozen in that anticipatory position, you instead will use the momentum of your upward swing to start the momentum of your downward swing. Immediately unwind all that energy built up in the twist of your body—first your hips begin moving back to the left, the hip movement's connected to your shoulder movement, the shoulder movement's connected to the arm movement, the arm movement's connected to the club movement, now hear the word of the Lord! (Oh, I'm sorry, I had a little spiritual reverie there, but I'm back now.) Let the club flow smoothly and easily back around toward the ball, letting your left arm pull the club. Your right hand's job is not to push, but merely to steady the club and left hand. Feel the shift of your weight, letting the other shoe drop, as it were, in finishing off your two-step.

All this time you are moving the club toward a rendezvous with the ball. Your club should be accelerating as you hit the ball. Your head should be down until after the ball is safely on its way. Follow through until your club is over your other shoulder in a near-mirror image of the position at the top of your swing, except that you'll be looking up watching your ball as it flies over the fairway, dives into the rough, or ricochets wildly from car to car in the parking lot.

When you practice on a driving range, try for a consistent swing that hits the ball squarely. After a while try shifting the club face slightly off square and see how even a subtle difference in angle as you swing can create a hook or slice. Learning to predict and control a hook or slice at will allows you to find the angle where you can hit without either; it also gives you a tool when curving the ball around an obstacle, like when a guy who got in the way of an earlier shot is lying unconscious on the fairway.

Golf Clubs

"There are long cleeks and short cleeks, driving cleeks, lofting cleeks, and putting cleeks; there are heavy irons and light irons, driving irons, lofting irons, and sand irons. There are mashies and niblicks. In this multitude of golf clubs there is wisdom—somewhere—but it can scarcely be that all of them are necessary."

—Horace Hutchinson, 1890

Cleeks? Mashies and niblicks? Ah, to have been around in those bygone, missing-links days when golf clubs had great names. Fitting the depersonalization of our times, modern day clubs mostly just come with numbers—a "3-iron," for example.

Also matching our times, the clubs come with a whole package of hype for all sorts of "new, improved" variations on those numbered clubs. New alloys and polymers, new shapes, different grooves, oxymorons like "metal woods" (but no wooden irons . . . yet), and more, all of which promise to straighten your slice, lengthen your drive, improve your loft and clear up your dandruff.

While there's no reason, except the limitations of money and storage space, not to try out any clubs that you think might improve your game, the reality is that you're better served trying to get good at playing well with any club instead of looking for the club that will magically fix your game. (If it really did do miracles, it would be ruled illegal

anyway, because golf is supposed to be a challenge. Otherwise, what's the point?)

If you're a beginner, you will most likely enjoy the game as much with used clubs from a garage sale as with a matching set made of the latest space-age polymers and alloys. (If nothing else, if you score badly you can always blame your equipment—try doing that when you have state-of-the-art everything.)

Because of golfers' propensity for falling for the latest new improvements in clubs, and because caddies were starting to get hernias from carrying dozens of weird specialty clubs, the golfing rules associations passed a rule early in this century limiting the number of clubs in your bag to a maximum of 14. In reality, though, a full set of clubs isn't even necessary: One expert suggests that beginners begin with as little as the 3-, 5-, 7- and 9-irons, a wedge and putter, a 5-wood, and a 3-wood for tee shots. You don't even necessarily have to buy clubs if you're not ready for the decision or the expense: Many courses will rent clubs, which is especially useful when traveling (unless, of course, you like to practice your putting in hotel rooms and your driving in deserted airport corridors.)

How Is Men's Equipment Different From Women's?

Yes, it sounds like the sort of question your 5-year-old might ask in a crowded elevator, but it is a valid one. Women's clubs are made shorter, lighter, cuter and with more flexible shafts. But that's less a role of gender than of body size. Small men might find a "women's" set of clubs best for them, and larger women may find "men's" equipment suitable for their needs.

What to Look For

All clubs have three major components: the head, shaft and

grip. How those work together are important to under-stand so that you can choose the elements that will make your clubs suit you and your game, and not vice versa. It used to be easier a few centuries back when all golf clubs were woods—hickory shaft, wooden head and a thick leather grip.

Getting the Shaft

The flexibility of a club's shaft is one variable you need to consider. The shaft of your club bends and twists slightly from centrifugal force and impact against the ball (or when you bang it against a tree in frustration). If you have a shaft that's too flexible for your swing, the ball will tend to hook. If not flexible enough, it will tend to slice. Weaker hitters should have a more flexible shaft; heavy hitters, a relative-ly inflexible shaft.

How can you tell a club's flexibility? Look for a label or decal on the club. Men's shafts come in four flexes: X for extra stiff; S for stiff; R for regular; and A for flexible. Women's come in two illogical designations: L for "ladies," which is stiffer than W for "women." (Actually, this might have made sense in the old days when people called an inflexibly upright female a "lady" and a loose-living female a "woman.")

Another measurement that affects the swing of your clubs is "swing weight," a scale that indicates how heavy a club feels when you swing it. It's a ratio that measures the interplay between the heaviness of your club head and the length of the shaft. Your golf clubs come with different lengths of shafts—if manufacturers used the same weight of club head for each, the clubs with the long shafts would feel heavier. They make the heads of short-shafted clubs proportionately heavier, to give all the clubs in your set the same "swing weight." Most men use a swing weight between a light C8 to a heavy D3. Most women's clubs range from a light C4 to a heavy C9.

Get a Grip

The grip on a golf club is usually either leather or rubber. Leather is classier, more traditional, more Republican, but rubber is easier to maintain, less slippery in wet weather and can better protect you from dreaded turf diseases that can crawl up the metal handles of golf clubs from playing on courses with Democrats and the aforementioned loose women.

The thickness of your grip changes the feel of your club. The thicker and heavier it is, the lighter the club head feels in comparison. Thick grips tend to restrict the movement of your hands and wrists, which is good if you have too much of either; thin grips tend to encourage movement, which is good if you have too little.

Heads You Win

Irons. There are two kinds of clubs, as you know—irons and woods. Irons are in fact made of steel, which is pretty gosh darn close to what they claim to be. (Steel, as everyone knows, is an alloy of iron, carbon and manganese, with nickel, chromium, and/or molybdenum sometimes thrown in for extra strength, color, flavor and preservatives.) They are either forged or cast. What's the difference? Forged clubs have been pulled from a hot fire and hammered out by hand, presumably by large mustachioed guys singing the *Anvil Chorus*. This is the traditional method. But with this method, the quality of the club depends on the skill of the blacksmith.

You can see why forged clubs have great appeal to golfers—bad shots can be blamed on the guy who made the club.

Cast iron heads are made in an even more exotic way—by using the "lost wax" method. This is a method that has been used for centuries by artists who sculpt in metal, and produces a nice, seamless casting. A model of each head is made of wax and a mold constructed around it. Molten metal is poured into the mold, which immediately melts the wax. After the wax is poured out of the mold, the liquid metal is poured in. The metal becomes solid as it cools, and the mold is removed from it. From there, the handle is attached using modern adhesives (in the old days, a rivet). In this way, a club head, once cast out of a ball of lost wax, begins a life of whacking and casting out lost balls.

Irons are typically used in the approach shots to the green from the fairway after you've hit the ball off the tee. But on holes of shorter distance, and depending on your abilities as a driver, you may find yourself using one of the irons directly off the tee.

Woods. You might expect that all woods are indeed made of wood. Ho, foolish earthling! Until the 1950s, woods were made of persimmon wood, which was hard and durable. However, thanks to role model Ike Eisenhower and postwar prosperity, the demand for golf clubs zoomed at a remarkable rate—so much so that the demand for quality persimmon wood far outstripped the supply. After trying inferior persimmon wood, which cracked and warped, manufacturers learned something from the lumber industry—that plywood is cheap and strong. They started using it, and many continue to do so today.

Even in the fruit salad days of persimmon, though, the heads were not 100% wood. More like 90%. Wood, after all, wears out and changes shape if you bang it often enough. Manufacturers responded by putting hard inserts into the face of the club—plastic, aluminum, even ivory. (As if the elephants weren't having enough trouble with encroachments on their habitats, they had to worry about being killed for the benefit of some guy's short game.)

More recently, manufacturers have come out with "metal woods." These are shaped like woods but are really a hollow metal shell (sometimes filled with polystyrene, presumably to dampen that telltale clang you hear with metal baseball bats). Although traditionalists find them to be an abomination against everything good and holy in golf (if there is, in fact, *anything* good and holy about golf), many pros like them for their paradise loft (11 degrees up and away off the fairway!) and many duffers like them because the clubhead doesn't twist as much around the shaft upon impact, creating an unnaturally straight shot.

The woods are typically used for the shots off the tee and on longer approach shots off the fairway to the green.

Club Sand Wedge?

"I asked my caddie for a sand wedge and he came back ten minutes later with a ham on rye."

—Chi Chi Rodriguez

What if baseball were like golf? A batter would say, "Well, I want to hit it low and hard between 2nd and 3rd. Whaddya think, a #4 aluminum?" It's a problem for new golfers: There are so many clubs to choose from, which do you use when?

In theory, it's not so hard. I say "in theory" because there are so many other variables in addition to the club that will affect where a golfer's shot will go. Let's pretend, in order to keep the theory intact, that none of the others apply—that you are going to hit every ball squarely and that your swing is not going to vary much in smoothness, power and precision.

Each club is designed to be slightly but significantly different from the one next to it in number and kind. So, let's take a 3-iron. It will—everything else being the same— whap the ball a little higher than a 2-iron, but not as high as a #4. The #3-launched ball (having gone higher than a ball hit with the #2) will not roll quite as far once it hits ground, but it will roll farther than one hit with a #4.

Let's say that you're a powerful golfer, and can regularly and accurately hit a ball 200 yards with a 1-wood (which is the club that gives the longest, lowest arc with the most roll, and is often referred to as the "driver"). The 3-wood would tend to give you about 190 yards with a slightly higher arc. The #5, about 180 yards. The 2-iron, 170 yards; the 3-iron, 160 yards; and so on through the irons, each number sacrificing about 10 yards of length for a correspondingly higher arc (and increasingly more control of where the ball will stop) until finally you get to #10, the "wedge," used to shoot you up and out of bunkers and other bad situations.

Chipping & Receiving
Sometimes you need to be able to get the ball from near the green to onto the green. A wood or most of the irons would obviously be "too much club" (Don't you love it when I talk golf language?) for the distance you want to go, yet a putt wouldn't get you far enough. That's when a "chip" comes in handy (maybe even a bag of chips, if you've had

the foresight to also pack a little tub of cool ranch-flavored dip in your golf bag).

What does "chipping" mean exactly? It's like a bunt in baseball—designed to hit the ball in a certain direction for a short distance. It's a shot that keeps to a low trajectory, spends only a little time in the air and then passes most of its life rolling along the ground. Hopefully, toward your target. As with a putt, it uses your arms and hands, and not your entire body as a drive does. Think of it as a mini-drive, a "Drive Lite"—you turn only slightly with your body, your back swing and follow-through only go halfway up, and you don't hit as hard; but otherwise your swing's essentially the same.

You stand slightly ahead of the ball , which is just about six inches off your right foot (Reverse these instructions, you lefties.), and your knees flexed to make it easier to get to the bottom of the ball when you hit it. Meanwhile, you lean your body to the left, almost to the point at which your right foot feels weightless, as if it could almost levitate off the ground.

When you swing, if you do it right, your club face doesn't pass your hands until the ball is well on its way. In this way, you hit with a nice descending blow.

Putting

"There are no points for style when it comes to putting. It's getting the ball in the cup that counts."

—Brian Swarbrick

Why is putting so important? Since usually about half your strokes will be on the green, it can be the great equalizer. Someone who isn't able to hit the long ball can often make up for it by outputting the long hitters.

Putting is sometimes called the "game within the game." Think of what golf would be with only greens, with no fairways, roughs, bunkers or long shots. Add some ramps, windmills, clown faces and funny obstacles, and what would you have? Miniature golf! It's such a great game to play with kids or other loved ones.

On the other hand, isn't one of the reasons for playing golf that you can get away from your loved ones for an afternoon? But I digress. Some say putting is the most important part of your game, pointing out that driving will get you onto the green but almost never into the hole. Others laugh bitterly, poke their fingers into your face and say that without a good drive, you'll have to putt a whole lot of strokes down the fairway from tee to cup.

Me, I just get a headache when people argue about things like this, and have to go away and lie down; or else I get a nosebleed. Can't we all just get along? Can't we just say that putting is important and get on with our lives?

Putting

Putters (I'm talking about the club now, not the people who putt.) come with a flat side on the top of the handle. There's a good reason for this. The flat side is there for your thumbs. The essence of putting is that you're going for maximum accuracy at a minimal distance. That's why most good putters (the people this time, not the club) modify their driving golf grip somewhat when putting. How much to modify is the question. Again, as in any art as full of science, arcane beliefs and outright superstition as golf is, there are a variety of right answers, all sworn to by their proponents as being the One True Answer. In putting, however, nearly all agree on one thing: Both thumbs go on the flat side of the handle.

Besides just using the same grip you use for driving (which some golfers do), there are two variations that are the most popular in the world of putting—the reverse overlap grip and the cross-handed grip. Whichever you use, the key is to hold the club firmly but lightly, never tightly. If you find yourself tensing your muscles, you are doing it wrong. Tensed muscles not only interfere with the fluid, easy swing you want, but they also block the sensations that your brain needs in order to feel and control the stroke you're about to make. So give it just enough muscle to hold onto the club and send the ball across the green, not enough to put your fingerprints into the handle and send the ball to the next tee.

Reverse Overlap Grip

You start by aligning your putter's face so that it is positioned right behind the ball and exactly perpendicular to the direction in which you want the ball to go. Then you position yourself and your hands to make that happen.

Your feet should be parallel with the intended path of the ball. Your left palm (Reverse these instructions if you're a lefty, of course.) goes exactly parallel to your putter's face as you place your hand near the end of your club's handle. Your left thumb points down, holding the flat side of the handle firmly but gently. Don't close your fingers around the club yet, just hold it in place with your thumb.

Put your right thumb just below your left thumb on the grip. Your open hands are parallel to each other and to the club face, with your right hand a few inches lower on the shaft than your left.

Okay, now close your right hand around the handle. Now, close your left hand. If you did it correctly, your left index finger is actually on top of your right pinkie. This feels strange, and still doesn't quite give the precision control that you want. We're going to make one more adjustment before you swing at your ball and putt it into the cup. Take that overlapping index finger and straighten it again, pivoting it down the shaft handle where it overlaps the fingers on your right hand. This helps keep your wrists from bending or flexing, which in putting is a good thing.

The Cross-Handed Grip

This is a newer grip designed to reduce the dominance of your stronger hand. Why do you want to do that? Experience shows that pulling the club with your left hand instead of pushing it with your right (if you're right-handed) is smoother and prevents certain jerks, uneven flutters and over-powering strokes that are built into the way the hand is constructed.

Essentially, you reverse the above instructions. Your right hand goes on first near the end of the handle, thumb on flat side of the handle. Your left hand goes below. As with the overlap grip, your hands can be overlapped or interlocked.

Putting

The Putting Stance

What's the most important part of your stance? Your eyes. That's true whether you're putting on a municipal golf course or putting on the Ritz.

Think of the ball as your Third Eye, the source of perception and inner wisdom in eastern philosophical thought. You want your two other eyes to be directly above it, aligned like three planets in an astrological trine denoting the harmony of the universe. The only difference between a golfer and a practitioner of yoga, of course, is that the yogi meditates on his Third Eye. You, my friend, on the other hand, are going to take a metal club and hit it.

The reason you want your eyes directly over your ball is that you want to see an undistorted straight line between

your eyes and the cup and feel confident that *that* is the line your ball is going to follow. Years of experience have taught golfers that if your eyes are positioned inside the plane of the ball, your putt will tend to go to the right of the cup (if you're right-handed) and that if your eyes are on the other side of the ball, not only will you be standing rather uncomfortably, but also your ball is likely to go to the left of the cup.

True, you can try allowing for that, but why bother? Do it right the first time and you won't regret it.

Okay, so if your eyes are above the ball, your body will have to work around that. First of all, realize that you'll be hunched over the ball, the top of your spine bent forward and horizontal. You know you're doing it right if you feel like Quasimodo in the bell tower. ("How did I know I'd putt so well? I had a hunch back on the green.") That isn't too hard, considering how short they make the putters.

Now you want to get very well balanced, because, unlike when driving the ball, you want to ensure that no part of your body will move when you putt except your arms. Your weight should be centered at the balls of your feet. (You might feel muscles in your calves, thighs and knees you haven't felt for years. Don't worry, it may hurt a little now, but be comforted by the fact that it will probably hurt even more tomorrow.) Your arms should, by virtue of your Quasimodo routine, be clear enough of your body to either ring a bell or swing a club cleanly without grazing any other part of your body. And your feet should be absolutely parallel with the line you hope your ball will travel, and not be spread too far apart—maybe a foot or so, at most. No pun intended.

Putting

Putt It in Its Place

Again, putting is where you have to unlearn a lot of what you learned in driving from the tee. Not only are your stance, grip and attitude different, but it's also a different type of swing. You use different muscles to control and propel the ball—muscles that are not so good for power-hitting but that are better for a smooth, predictable, accurate stroke.

As in the choice of grips, professionals use one of two completely contradictory options when putting. Either one works. Both require that you keep your body and head absolutely still and your eyes over the ball. Try both of them and see which better matches your game and personality. Personality? Sure. "You can tell people's innermost being by the way they play golf," swears a psychiatrist who plays twice a week (and who actually sometimes recruits patients from his fellow players). He says that "choppy putters" (those who use jab strokes) are angrier and more impatient than "smooth putters" (those who use sweeping strokes). I'm sure you can imagine what kind of putts the good doctor prefers.

Sweeping Stroke

Favored by most professionals, the sweep stroke uses very little wrist movement. Instead, the arms and shoulders make a wide, slow arc that guides the ball toward the cup, slowing as it approaches so that it just dribbles in. The forward follow-though is about as long as the backstroke—both of which get longer when the putt has to travel a longer distance. The advantage of the sweeping stroke is that it keeps the putter closer to the ground and keeps the face of your club from rotating all the way through the stroke, increasing your chance of guiding the ball to where you want it. Also, because the club, and therefore the ball, goes more slowly than with a jab stroke, you're closer to the cup in case (heaven forbid!) you miss.

Jab Stroke

The jab stroke is almost the opposite of the sweep stroke. You use your wrists and keep your arms and shoulders still. You "jab" at the ball in a short spastic motion reminiscent of swatting a fly, or hammering a tack, without following through. Finally, you hit the ball harder, so it will tend to bounce off the back rim into the hole like a basketball off a backboard . . . or, if you miss, will tend to end up farther afield.

You want to keep your head down and absolutely still until the ball is safely on its way. That can be hard on a long putt, because the hole will be outside of your field of vision. What you want to do, as in driving, is to find a spot midway between you and the hole along the path you want your ball to travel, and aim for it.

Earth, Wind and Fire

Let's pretend that you've somehow achieved every golfer's dream: a clean and powerful drive and an accurate and reliable putt. So how come you're still not scoring that well?

The problem lies not in your skills, but in the lay of the land. A near-perfect aim in itself is great—as long as you're playing on a straight and level course on a windless day. That doesn't happen often, however. On every hole you'll have to deal with the imperfections of an imperfect world. Just remember: Any time you're fighting against gravity, wind, earth or trees, you're bound to lose. So rather than fight the powers of the universe, work with them. Let's take them one by one.

Over Hill, Over Dale

One of the frustrations of hitting what normally would be a great shot in golf is in watching the ball suddenly begin rolling in an unexpected, unwanted direction as it follows the contours of the land. So when driving—and especially when putting—you need to allow for curves and inclines.

For example, if you're hitting on a green that slants to the right, you need to aim for a spot somewhat to the left of the hole, far enough that the ball will curve toward (and into) the hole when it "breaks" (is affected by the terrain). As in bowling, that'll happen more toward the end of the ball's path than at the beginning, tending to make a "J" shape as the ball slows down, is affected by your stroke less and by the lay of the land more. So pay special attention to the last yard or so approaching the hole. Whether it's a good break or a bad break depends on how well you "read" the green and allowed for its idiosyncrasies and imperfections.

It gets more complicated if the hill is, for example, inclined to one side and toward you, as well. Or if it slants to the left and then to the right. (Ever try to guide a ball in an "S" shape?) It means having to allow for all the factors (bearing in mind that your ball will be affected more at the end of its path than at its beginning) and trying to figure out exactly where to aim so as to work with the terrain.

Many pros go through a ritual when scoping out a complicated putt—looking low from behind the ball to see the land from the ball's point of view, walking around to behind the cup to see what it looks like from there, and then circling around back to where they started before hitting the ball. On the other hand, it's also easy to overcompensate for the hills and ridges and even the "grain" of the way the grass is growing. If you get confused and don't quite know what to do, fall back on your common sense: Hit the ball straight for the cup. Even with the effects of hill and dale, you'll end up close to where you want to go; and if you pay attention to the way the ball breaks, you'll learn something useful for the next shot, and for the next time you're on a similar hole.

Wind

Here's a quick meteorological lesson: According to scientists, the wind is not, as most people suppose, air being *pushed* from somewhere to somewhere else. It is in fact being *pulled* as with a vacuum cleaner. What typically happens is that the sun heats the air in one geographic location more than in another. The heated air rises, pulling cooler, heavier air from cooler areas around it. (This is why prevailing winds usually travel from large bodies of water to inland areas.) To put it bluntly, the wind doesn't blow, it actually suctions. Even though the general public doesn't know this, most golfers do. Hang around any tee on a blustery day and you'll hear a great deal of elaboration on how the wind sucks.

It's important to not let yourself get blown over (or suckered) by the wind. I mean that literally, of course, but also figuratively: It's a mistake to try to fight the wind instead of using it to your advantage.

How do you use the wind? Well, if it's at your back, lay off your stroke a bit, use a higher-hitting club like a 3-wood, tee your ball up a little higher than normal, and loft the ball up into the air. The wind will do some of your work for you. If the wind is blowing straight at you, don't try to murder your ball; just take a full swing and keep your ball's loft low. Remember that a wind at your back will tend to straighten out any hook or slice you might have; a wind at your front will make it worse.

If you're playing against a crosswind, try to anticipate how far to the side your ball is going to travel in the wind and aim at a point that many feet upwind.

Rain

While we're talking about bad weather, let's mention rain. If you're enough of a fanatic to want to play on a course in which everything is a water hazard, remember that the rain will affect your play in countless ways. Let's count a few of them:

1. Your vision. If you wear glasses, make sure you wear a big-brimmed hat, or you won't see much of anything. Even if you don't wear glasses, rain makes it difficult to see.

2. Your spin. You might find that the ball is traveling about two yards farther than usual. That's because the water is lubricating the head of your club where it hits the ball, reducing or even eliminating the amount of spin. The effect is like a knuckle ball in baseball—wobbly and unpredictable. Many clubs now have squared grooves that eliminate or reduce this.

3. Roll. Your ball won't continue to roll as far in wet grass as in dry.

4. Sand traps. The good news is that rain packs down the sand and renders bunkers fairly harmless. You can often chip the ball off the surface as if it were on the fairway.

5. Lightning. A golf course is *almost* the last place you want to be in a lightning storm because you'll likely be the tallest thing standing there—a sort of lightning rod. Under a tree on a golf course *is* the last place you want to be. Every so often golfers with more fanaticism than sense are propelled off this mortal green by God's chip shot. If you hear thunder in the distance, think of it as a divine "Fore!" and retire to the clubhouse to let Him (or Her) play through.

Lee Trevino was hit by lightning during the second round of the Western Open golf tournament in 1975. When asked if he had any advice on how other players could avoid being hit, he said: "Hold up a 1-iron and walk. Even God can't hit a 1-iron."

Having a Ball

"The golfer will never settle for anything. He's too insecure. The golfer is a crazy guy. One stroke means more than his mother to him. If he thinks a new ball will go a 20th of an inch longer, that's his ball."
— Dave Lumley, Wilson Marketing Director

Manufacturers make more than 500 million golf balls a year. Since there aren't near enough new golfers to account for that figure, you can imagine how many of those end up lost forever in lakes, roughs, forests and the windows of turfside condominiums.

The first golf ball was made by the Romans for the game they called *"paganica."* It was made of feathers wrapped in leather and would go as far as 150 yards if you really walloped it. The process for making the ball got only a little more refined over the centuries. In Scotland during the early days of "gawf," ball makers wetted a hatful of chicken or goose feathers with a solution of alum and water, then stuffed and stitched them into a leather cover, a two-hour process. That ball could go 180 yards.

It wasn't until 1848 that the first major bounce in golf ball technology came along. Nine years after Charles Goodyear first vulcanized rubber, the first rubber golf ball flew off a tee and into the sandtraps of history. It was called the *"gutta percha,"* after the rubber tree in Malaysia. (The name means "gum tree" in Malay . . . and golfers have been

playing the ball where it Malays—and even in a malaise—
ever since.) The *gutta percha's* main advantage was that it
was cheaper and more durable than the feather/leather ball.

In 1899, *gutta perchas* were replaced by "bounding bil-
lies"—a small rubber core wrapped with rubber bands and
covered with a *gutta percha* skin. A few years later, a more
durable skin was made with a rubber from South America
called *"balata."*

About that time, scientists began solving a mystery that
had bedeviled golfers for half a century: Why didn't *gutta
percha* balls travel only as far as feather balls when they
were new, but could soar 60% further when they got old?
At first they thought that maybe rubber got more bouncy
as it aged, but research disproved that. Finally, someone
realized that it was because of nicks and scratches on the
ball. The spin of a nicked ball provided lift like the wing of
an airplane (which hadn't been invented yet). The ball also
flew more accurately.

That was the beginning of some trial-and-error attempts
to find the optimal surface pattern. A mesh pattern and a
bumpy one that looked like a bad case of acne were the first
attempts. Finally, in 1908, pimples gave way to dimples.
That did the trick, and the ball remained essentially
unchanged for another half-century.

In the 1960s, DuPont came out with a new thermoplas-
tic material called "Surlyn" that resisted the service cuts
that occurred when balls were clubbed badly. Most balls
sold today are Surlyn-covered, although most championship golfers still use *balata* because it makes the ball spin
more and stop faster.

In 1968, Spalding created the "two piece ball" which
got rid of the rubber bands, using a solid plastic center with

a Surlyn cover. It flew higher and further, and grabbed a large chunk of the ball market.

A few years later, the ball companies began looking for a new gimmick. They started thinking like the casting director for a 1930s musical and decided that the more dimples, the better. In 1983, Titlist made a ball with 392 dimples, which was quickly matched by Hogan. In 1984, Spalding fought back with a 492 dimple ball; not long after, Bridgestone came out with one that they claimed had 318 tiny dimples inside 318 larger dimples. The Dimple Race came to a head when Acushnet sued Spalding in 1990, claiming that Spalding had copied its patented dimple design. How far did golf balls go into indented servitude? The stats tell the story: In 1983, the average ball had 330 dimples. In 1995, it had 415.

Does the increased number of dimples help? Some golfers swear by them. But despite all the hoopla and high-tech gibberish, the technicians and statisticians in the United States Golf Association have found no evidence that today's golf balls actually travel significantly further than they did 20 years ago. The USGA keeps careful watch on the claims of new equipment. One USGA rule is that balls fly no faster than 255 feet per second off the club head, nor travel more than 280 yards off the USGA automated swing machine. In addition, the golf ball must be at least 1.68 inches in diameter and weigh no more than 1.62 ounces.

Clearly, the premium prices of the new balls show that listening to ad claims and golf folklore can cost you money. But it can cost you more than that. Just ask Mark Minnie of San Jose, California. A few years ago, when Minnie was 17 years old, he heard a radio DJ claim that a hot golf ball will go further than a cold one. Minnie took the advice to heart and nuked a golf ball in his mom's microwave. The ball exploded, covering the inside of the oven with molten rubber and permeating the house with the lingering scent of Eau de Akron.

"Every manufacturer is jumping on the bandwagon and trying to get a niche in the market to satisfy every golfer's need," says one golf pro. "But the average player can pick up a no-name brand at $15.99 for 15 balls and get as much out of them as spending $28 for a dozen brand-name balls and not knowing what to do with them."

Country Clubs

There is one nagging problem with playing golf that goes beyond a hook or a slice. All too often, public courses can be crowded and undermaintained, leaving you to consider the option of joining a club. Besides being extremely expensive, country clubs have an image of stuffy exclusivity that is sadly true in many cases. What do you think of belonging to an organization that still—even as we are about to enter the 21st century—excludes racial minorities and Jews and doesn't allow women to be full members, restricting their golf attire and making them play only at narrowly limited times? Even halfway reasonable Americans would be appalled by such blatant sexism and racism, yet a large number of country clubs continue to practice discriminatory policies that civilized institutions in this country abandoned at least three decades ago.

Members somehow find themselves able to rationalize belonging to them. ("Oh, they don't discriminate, it's just that no African-Americans were ever accepted as members.") And to be fair, some country clubs actively practice a more enlightened philosophy. But this may be an issue you want to ask about when considering membership.

Dress

"Very few blacks will take up golf until the requirement for plaid pants is dropped."
—Franklin Ajaye, African-American comedian

Figuring how to dress when you go golfing is no small consideration. Many golfers pride themselves on bad taste, and if you want to join them, hey, it's a free country. But be aware that many courses have official or unofficial clothing rules.

If you want to play it safe when going to a course for the first time, either call in advance and ask or go conservative. For men that means golf shoes, preppy slacks and collared sport shirts (probably not Hawaiian prints for your first showing, no matter how muted the fluorescent colors). Women no longer have to play in long full skirts, petticoats and bustles, as they did in the 1870s, but a conservative shirt with slacks, skirts or shorts is never out of place.

Tam o' shanters, alas, are still popular with some crowds, although not quite the fashion statement they once were. Baseball caps, whether worn brim front or back, are strictly frowned on, regardless of the team. Still, some kind of hat is a good idea to protect you from the rays of the sun (and partially mask your identity if you hit a bystander with an errant drive).

Many courses, you'll find, allow men to play in shorts. But not just any shorts, mind you. Tennis shorts or running shorts are forbidden on most courses.

A different kind of logic governs shoes. Golf shoes aren't always required, but are always welcome. Greens are very tender things, so cowboy boots, high heels, most running shoes, galoshes, snow shoes, etc. are barred. Lenient courses allow tennies or other soft-soled shoes, but I wouldn't try going barefoot.

Etiquette

Many rules in golf are written down. In fact, some say too many of them. Some of them, however, are unwritten, but you would do well to observe them.

• A cough at the right moment can throw a golfer off enough to miss a crucial money-winning putt. So can jingling your keys, clearing your throat or otherwise issuing sudden noises or movements. And it's best to not even appear in a fellow golfer's peripheral vision. (A good caddie, for example, will stand several yards directly behind the golfer.)

• Leave the cellular phone in the car. If you absolutely must have it with you (to give your boss or clients the impression that you're at work, for example) keep the conversation short and don't hold up play. If your phone rings in the middle of a crucial putt, it's going to be hard to convince your opponent that you didn't furtively page a confederate to call you back at just that inopportune (or opportune) moment.

• Replace your divots. Nobody wants to have to clean up, or play out of, a mess you've left; so unless you've invited your mom to be part of your foursome, leave no mess behind. (Not only good etiquette on the golf course, but also a good metaphor for living a grown-up life.)

• If you must use a golf cart (which is pretty unnecessary, unless you're physically unable to walk), keep it on the paths, off the grass, and far away from anyone concentrating on that next shot.

• Don't wait to be asked to put down a marker if you're the closest to the hole.

• Stay off the other players' "putting lines," the space between their ball and the hole. Your light footprint in the grass can be enough to affect the roll of their ball in a subtle but crucial way, so don't even risk being a convenient target for blame.

Golf Jokes

If you play golf long enough (Two weeks is about right.), you'll hear most of the same golf jokes over and over again. Worst of all, most of them have the same subtext—the idea that golfers are so obsessed by the game that they value it more than anything or anybody else.

Here are some of the best of the lot. You can try telling them to your golf buddies. Best of all, though, is that when a member of your foursome starts telling a joke between the sixth and seventh hole and says, "Stop me if you've heard this one," you can most likely cover your ears and scream, "STOP!"

Not that it'll do any good, of course. The only thing that will really stop a golfer in the middle of a golf story is a 4-iron to the head.

Golfing with his regular foursome, Joe suddenly stopped playing. He took his hat off and placed it over his heart at the funeral procession going by. Afterward, one of his partners complimented Joe on his thoughtfulness. "What else could I do?" replied Joe solemnly. "Sunday would have been our 35th wedding anniversary."

Tom was playing golf with his wife. He hit his shot into the woods left of the fairway, and it landed near a storage shed.

He was about to chip out onto the fairway when his wife

said: "If I stand behind the door and hold it open, you can aim through the window in back and get the ball up on the green. Easy shot, you can do it."

She stood behind the door, he set up the shot and hit it almost perfectly . . . but not perfectly enough. The ball caromed off the window frame and hit his wife on the head, killing her instantly.

After years of therapy, Tom decided to play the same course again. To his horror, he hit his ball into exactly the same spot. He prepared to chip out onto the fairway again when his playing partner suggested: "If I stand behind the door and hold it open, you can aim through the window in back and get the ball up on the green . . . ."

"No way!" Tom screamed hysterically. "The last time I tried that shot I took a double bogey!"

A hack golfer gets more and more depressed as he plays the game poorly all day. At the 18th hole, he spots a lake off the fairway. He tells the caddie, "I've played so poorly all day, I think I'll go drown myself in that lake." The caddie responds, "I'm not worried—I don't think you could keep your head down that long."

A man came home from playing golf and announced to his wife, "I'm never playing golf with Bill ever again."

"Why not?" she asked. "He's been your friend for years."

"Would you continue to play with a guy who always gets drunk, loses so many balls that other groups are always playing through, tells lousy jokes while you are trying to putt and generally offends everyone around him on the course?"

"Certainly not," she replied.

"Well, neither would Bill."

Bob couldn't find his golf ball. Finally, out of desperation, he snuck a new ball out of his pocket and dropped it on the ground when his partner wasn't looking. "Dave, I've found it!" he yelled.

Dave exploded: "You cheater! How dare you! I never thought you'd stoop to cheating for a mere dollar!"

"What do you mean 'cheater'?" Bob said indignantly. "I found my ball, I'll play it where it lies!"

"I can prove that's not your ball, you SOB," screamed Dave triumphantly, "because I've been standing on your ball for five minutes!"

A golfer is so bad that he's embarrassed to be seen playing; so he decides to practice early in the morning so that nobody will see him. One morning he tees up the ball and hits it. The ball slices viciously and flies out of sight over the golf club fence. He's so depressed he packs up his stuff and goes home.

The next day he tries again. Again he slices the ball over the fence, but this time the ball narrowly misses a man walking his dog. The golfer rushes over to the man, apologizing as he goes.

"You were here yesterday and did the same thing, didn't you?" the dog owner asks. "Did you see where yesterday's ball ended up?"

"No," says the golfer.

"It bounced onto the main road, shattered a car's windshield, and caused it to skid into a wall. The driver was killed instantly."

"That's terrible," exclaims the golfer. "What can I do?"

"You want to keep your head down and stop dropping your left shoulder."

⤸

"How did golf go?" asked the wife.

"It was terrible," said the golfer. "Halfway through the fourth hole, my old friend George collapsed from a massive coronary and died."

"That's horrible!" said the wife.

"You're telling me!" said the golfer. "All day long it was hit the ball, drag George, hit the ball, drag George."

⤸

A woman was out golfing, and a wasp stung her. After finishing the round, she went to the golf pro to get some advice about her driving. She mentioned the sting she'd gotten.

"Where were you stung?" he asked.

"Between the first and second hole," she said.

"Ah, I know your problem," the pro said. "Your stance is too wide."

⤸

A woman asked her husband: "If I died, would you marry again?"

"Probably," he said.

"And would you let her come into my house?"

"Probably."

"Would she sleep in my bed?"

"Probably."

"Would she wear my jewelry?"

"Probably."

"Would she use my golf clubs?"

"No, definitely not."

"How sweet. Why not?"

"She's left-handed."

A minister played hooky from his congregation one Sunday and went golfing by himself. God and St. Peter looked down, and Peter said, "Look at him. He lied to his congregation telling them he was sick, and here he is playing golf on Sunday morning. What will you do?"

God said, "I'll punish him." The minister teed off and immediately got a hole in one. He looked around for witnesses at the empty course around him. Not finding any, he went on to the next hole, where exactly the same thing happened—a hole in one.

"What was that all about?" asked Peter, shaking his head at the mysterious ways of the Lord. "I thought you were going to punish him!"

"I just did," said God. "Who's going to believe him?"

Jesus and God the Father are playing golf. Jesus hits first and drives the ball down the middle of the fairway. God goes next and hits a little duck hook off into the woods. Just as the ball is about to stop rolling, a squirrel picks it up in its mouth and begins to run down the fairway. About halfway to the hole, the squirrel tires and is about to stop when an eagle swoops down out of the sky, sinks its talons into the squirrel's back and flies off with it. As the eagle flies high above the green, it squeezes the squirrel's back, causing it to open its mouth. The ball falls a thousand feet straight into the cup. God looks at Jesus. Jesus looks at God. Finally Jesus says, "You want to play golf or you want to screw around?"

A priest and a nun went golfing. The nun teed off and hit it straight toward the green. The priest's ball went right into the woods. "Oh $%#@! I missed!" he shouted.

"Father! Watch your language, " said the nun. "The Lord would not like that."

He next hit his ball into a sand trap.

He shouted, "Oh $%#@! I missed!"

"Father!" said the nun. "Watch what you say! Think of God."

The priest wedged his ball neatly out of the bunker . . . and right into a water hazard.

He shouted, "Oh $%#@! I missed!"

As the nun opened her mouth to rebuke him once again, a great bolt of lightning ripped down from the sky and struck her, reducing her to a little pile of ashes.

From the sky came a deafening, booming voice: "OH, $%#@! I MISSED!"

Two golfers were being held up as the twosome of women in front of them whiffed shots, hunted for lost balls and stood over putts for what seemed like hours.

"I'll ask if we can play through," Bill said as he strode toward the women.

Twenty yards from the green, however, he turned on his heel and went back to where his companion was waiting.

"Can't do it," he explained, sheepishly. "One of them's my wife and the other's my mistress!"

"I'll ask," said Jim. He started off, only to turn and come back before reaching the green.

"What's wrong?" Bill asked.

"Small world, isn't it?" said Jim.

Standing on the tee of a relatively long par three, the confident golfer said to his caddie, "Looks like a 4-wood and a putt to me." The caddie handed him the 4-wood, which he topped about 15 yards off the front of the tee. Immediately the caddie handed him his putter and said, "And now for one hell of a putt."

"I just got a new set of golf clubs for my husband," says the woman to her friend.

"Gee, what a great trade," replies the friend.

For most of the round the golfer had argued with his caddie about club selection. Finally on the 17th hole, a 185-yard par three into the wind, the caddie handed the golfer a 4-wood and the golfer balked.

"I think it's a 3-iron," said the golfer.

"No, sir it's a 4-wood," said the caddie. "A 3-iron won't hit it far enough."

"Nope, it's definitely a 3-iron."

So the golfer took the 3-iron and struck the ball perfectly. It tore through the wind, hit softly on the front of the green, and rolled up two feet short of the pin.

"See," said the caddie. "I told you it wasn't enough club."

Sue stood over her tee shot on the 18th hole for what seemed like forever. Finally, Mary, her playing partner, asked, "Why on earth are you taking so long to make this shot?"

"My husband is up there watching me from the clubhouse, and I want to make this shot a good one," said Sue.

"You're going about it all wrong," said Mary. "Unless you use a 3-wood and turn around, there's no way you're going to hit him from here."

Strokes of Genius

"Golf is the most over-taught and least-learned human endeavor. If they taught sex the way they teach golf, the race would have died out years ago." —*Jim Murray*

"When you watch a game, it's fun; when you play a game, it's recreation; but when you work at a game, it's golf." —*Bob Hope*

"I don't like golf. When I hit a ball, I want somebody else to chase it." —*Rogers Hornsby*

"In baseball, you can hit your home run over the right-field or center-field or left-field fence. In golf, everything has to be right over second base." —*Ken Harrelson*

"I am curiously, disproportionately, undeservedly happy on a golf course." —*John Updike*

"It is almost impossible to remember how tragic a place the world is when one is playing golf." —*Robert Lynd*

"Pick up the ball and have the clubs destroyed immediately." —*Viscount Castleross to his caddie after a series of bad shots*

"Ambition is a grievous fault . . . and grievously doth the duffer pay." —*William Shakespeare*

"Give me golf clubs, fresh air and a beautiful partner, and you can keep my golf clubs and the fresh air."

—*Jack Benny*

"Golf is the most fun you can have without taking your clothes off."
—*Chi Chi Rodriguez*

"The uglier a man's legs are, the better he plays golf. It's almost a law."
—*H. G. Wells*

"Prayer never works for me on the golf course. That may have something to do with my being a terrible putter."
—*The Rev. Billy Graham*

"The least thing upsets him on the links. He misses short putts because of the uproar of the butterflies in the adjoining meadows."
—*P. G. Wodehouse*

"It is impossible to imagine Goethe or Beethoven being good at billiards or golf."
—*H. L. Mencken*

"The more I see of golf, the more it reminds me of life. Or, rather, the more I see of life, the more it reminds me of golf."
—*Henry Longhurst*

"Golf is an expensive way of playing marbles."
—*G. K. Chesterton*

"Isn't it fun to get out on the golf course and lie in the sun?"
—*Bob Hope*

"It's good sportsmanship not to pick up golf balls while they are still rolling."   —*Mark Twain*

"One of the very important attractions of golf is that it provides a wide and varied assortment of topics for conversation."   —*Bobby Jones*

"If you want to take long walks, take long walks. If you want to hit things with a stick, hit things with a stick. But there's no excuse for combining the two and putting the results on TV. Golf is not so much a sport as an insult to lawns."
—*National Lampoon*

"The arc of your swing doesn't have a thing to do with the size of your heart."
—*Carol Mann*

"The place of the father in the modern suburban family is a very small one, particularly if he plays golf."
—*Bernard Russell*

"Golf is a good walk spoiled."
—*Mark Twain*

Strokes of Genius

"I use the word 'bunker,' meaning a pit in which the soil has been exposed and the area covered with sand. I regard the term 'sand trap' as an unacceptable Americanization. Its use annoys me almost as much as hearing a golf club called a 'stick.' Earthworks, mounds and the like, without sand, are not 'bunkers.'"

—*course designer Bob Jones*

"Golfers can survive slumps better than boxers. If boxers have a bad streak, they get knocked on their cans."

—*Tom Watson*

"If I had my way, any man guilty of golf would be ineligible for any office of trust in the United States."

—*H. L. Mencken*

"The beauty of golf stems from the fact that success, as well as failure, comes from within."

—*Tom Watson*

Wannabe Guide to Golf

"The mind messes up more shots than the body."
—*Tommy Bolt*

"It matters not whether you win or lose; what matters is whether I win or lose."
—*Darin Weinberg*

"It took me 17 years to get 3,000 hits in baseball. I did it in one afternoon on the golf course."
—*Hank Aaron*

"Why am I using a new putter? Because the old one didn't float too well."
—*Craig Sandler*

"Old golfers never die. They just lose their balls."
—*Bumper sticker*

"The hardest shot in golf? I find it to be the hole in one."
—*Groucho Marx*

"Golf giveth and golf taketh away, but it taketh away a hell of a lot more than it giveth."
—*Simon Hobday*

"Golf is a game of inches. The most important are those between the ears."
—*Arnold Palmer*

"I never really dreamed of making many putts. Maybe that's why I haven't made many."
—*Calvin Peete*

"The worst club in my bag is my brain." —*Chris Perry*

"Golf is the Lord's punishment for man's sins."
—*James Reston*

Strokes of Genius

"There are two reasons for making a hole in one. The first is that it is immensely laborsaving." —*H.I. Phillips*

"I was three over—one over a house, one over a patio and one over a swimming pool." —*George Brett*

"I've heard of unplayable lies, but on the tee?" —*Bob Hope*

"Golf is a game with the soul of a 1956 Rotarian." —*Bill Mandel*

"The golf swing is like sex: You can't be thinking of the mechanics of the act while you're doing it." —*Dave Hill*

"That little white ball won't move 'til you hit it, and there's nothing you can do after it's gone." —*Babe Didrickson Zaharias*

"If you are going to throw a club, it is important to throw it ahead of you, down the fairway, so you don't have to waste energy going back to pick it up." —*Tommy Bolt*

"Never break your putter and driver in the same match, or you're dead." —*Tommy Bolt*

"If the following foursome is pressing you, wave them through—and then speed up." —*Dean Beman*

"Being left-handed is a big advantage: No one knows enough about your swing to mess you up with advice." —*Bob Charles*

"Golf is second only to Christianity, and is its greatest ally in the development of the highest standard of American manhood and womanhood."
—*Rev. Dr. Paul Arnold Peterson*

"Golf is a game where guts and blind devotion will always get you absolutely nothing but an ulcer."
—*Tommy Bolt*

"I play with friends, but we don't play friendly games."
—*Ben Hogan*

"I'm hitting the woods just great, but I'm having a terrible time getting out of them." —*Harry Tofcano*

"If there is any larceny in man, golf will bring it out."
—*Unknown*

"The harder you work, the luckier you get."
—*Gary Player*

"The fun you get from golf is in direct ratio to the effort you don't put into it." —*Bob Allen*

"Most golfers prepare for disaster. A good golfer prepares for success." —*Bob Toski*

"A lot of guys who have never choked have never been in the position to do so." —*Tom Watson*

"Never bet with anyone you meet on the first tee, who

has a deep suntan, a 1-iron in his bag and squinty eyes."
—*Dave Marr*

"If you want to beat someone out on the golf course, just get him mad." —*Dave Williams*

"Real golfers don't cry when they line up their fourth putt." —*Unknown*

"If you try to fight the course, it will beat you."
—*Lou Graham*

"Putts get real difficult the day they hand out the money." —*Lee Trevino*

"It's nice to have the opportunity to play for so much money, but it's nicer to win it." —*Patty Sheenan*

"You've just got one problem. You stand too close to the ball after you've hit it."

—*Sam Snead*

"Lay off for three weeks, and then quit for good."
—*Sam Snead*

"Take it easy and lazily, because the golf ball isn't going to run away from you while you're swinging."
—*Sam Snead*

"Golf is an ideal diversion, but a ruinous disease."
—*Bertie Charles Forbes*

"Golf is the hardest game in the world to play, and the

easiest to cheat at."   —*Dave Hill*

"In golf as in life, it's the follow through that makes the difference."   —*Unknown*

"If you think it's hard to meet new people, try picking up the wrong golf ball."   —*Jack Lemmon*

"Golf is 20 percent mechanics and technique. The other 80 percent is philosophy, humor, tragedy, romance, melodrama, companionship, cama- raderie, cussedness and conversation"
—*Grantland Rice*

Strokes of Genius

"As you walk down the fairway of life you must smell the roses, for you only get to play one round."

—*Ben Hogan*

"Golf is a game whose aim is to hit a very small ball into an even smaller hole, with weapons singularly ill-designed for the purpose."

—*Winston Churchill*

Great Moments, Great Golfers

There are certain great golfers that you may hear references to in the clubhouse and bar. Here's a quick lesson on some of the most notable golfers:

Francis ("Frankie") Ouimet

Ouimet started an American golf craze in 1913 when, as a gangly 20-year-old, he came from nowhere and in the U.S. Open, beat the two best golfers in the world, Britons Harry Vardon and Ted Red. The tournament took place on a course he knew well, both as a player and a 28-cents-an-hour caddie, and he used that home-links advantage, as well as a deliberate, careful playing style, to defeat both champions. He never went pro, but his amateur status was briefly rescinded in 1914, back when people took amateur status seriously, because of his association with a sporting goods manufacturer.

Walter Hagen

Hagen won 11 major championships beginning in 1914. Besides being a great player, he had a colorful image that did much to bring professional golf to public consciousness. He spent his winnings as fast as he earned them, overtipping waiters, hatcheck girls and others during the Roaring '20s. (More than once, he turned over his entire winning check to a particularly helpful or friendly caddie.) At one posh country club he was told that as a "mercenary" pro golfer, he couldn't change clothes in the clubhouse, so he hired a stretch limousine to park at the front gate. He changed in the car, and at the end of the day had the driver meet him on the 18th hole with a polo coat.

Hagen was a master of psychological warfare against opponents and is credited, or blamed, with creating the outlandishly colored golf fashions that still afflict us. "That was done to get my opponent's eyes and mind off the ball," he explained later. "When the boys saw me, it reminded them of a sunset, plus some additional pastels. It used to make them a bit dizzy, and while they were dizzy, I took a hole or two." To distract opponent Gene Sarazen at the U.S. Open in 1922, he sent him an incredibly garish orange plaid tie with an anonymous mash note reading, "You probably don't remember me, but I'm that blond you met from the *Follies*. Don't look for me in the gallery, I don't want you to take your mind off Hagen. But wear this tie for good luck." Hagen spent the day razzing the chivalrous Sarazen for wearing such an ugly tie, but in the end, despite the tie and watching the gallery for a mysterious blond, Sarazen won the tournament.

Gene Sarazen
He first made a splash at age 20 by beating Walter Hagen in the 1922 U.S. Open. He won his seventh major victory at the Masters in 1935 with a double eagle on the par-5, 485-yard 15th hole at Augusta, Georgia, when he landed the ball in the cup from 235 yards away.

Bobby Jones
Regarded as the foremost amateur player in history, Jones

started playing golf with his parents at age 5 (but preferred fishing and baseball because "golf's too slow"). In 1923, he began winning championships, and in 1930 he won a Grand Slam of both the U.S. and British Amateur Open championships, a stunning achievement that was golfing's equivalent to Babe Ruth hitting 60 home runs in 1927. Two months later, having no further mountains to climb, he retired. He made instructional movies, wrote books and founded the Masters tournament in 1933, which he hosted until 1967.

Mildred "Babe" Didrickson Zaharias

An all-around athlete at a time when women's sports were barely in existence, Zaharias made her fame in the 1932 Olympic track and field competitions in which she took gold medals in the 80-meter hurdles and javelin throw and tied for a gold medal in the high jump, but was then disqualified for using the head-first leap that is now standard. Afterward, she took up baseball, pitching an inning as a temporary member of the Brooklyn Dodgers and another time striking out Joe DiMaggio. She tried football with the Southern Methodist University team, won fly-casting contests and competed honorably in softball, swimming and bowling.

Finally, she decided to try golf. The first time she ever swung a club, she shot a 43 for nine holes and quickly excelled at banging out 250-yard drives. In 1946 and '47 she gained 15 consecutive tournament victories, including the British Ladies Open. She died of cancer in 1956 at age 42, while still in the top rank of golfers.

Ben Hogan

A championship golfer in the 1940s, Hogan nearly died in a five-car crash in 1949. Doctors didn't believe that he'd walk again.

Hogan, however, in a display of will and disdain for crippling pain, began golfing again after a year of recovery. He lost his first comeback match to a young Sam Snead but in 1953 had his best year yet and played professionally into the 1970s, winning the U.S. Open four times, a record that stands to this day.

Patty Berg

One of the founders of the Ladies Professional Golf Association, Berg was a leading player in the league from the 1940s into the 1960s. She was one of Babe Zaharias' best friends and toughest rivals over the years. She won seven Title Holders competitions, seven Western Opens, four World Championships and three Vare Trophies.

Arnold Palmer

Appearing just in time for network TV in 1954, the ruggedly handsome Palmer became the Elvis of the links, the most popular golfer ever. He was friendly and personable to fans; and on TV, he was even expressive enough to come across on those tiny little black and white screens. Starting with an amazing comeback victory in the 1960 U.S. Open, Palmer dominated the PGA in the early 1960s, winning nearly everything in sight, and becoming a multimillionaire in short order between his golf winnings and marketing of Arnold Palmer equipment, clothes, golf bags and even a record album, *Arnold Palmer's Music for Swingin' Golfers*. In 1980, he joined the fledgling PGA Senior Tour and won the Senior Skins match three times between 1990 and 1996.

Jack Nicklaus

Called the "golden bear," for his size, temperament and winnings, Nicklaus won the 1959 National Amateur competition at the age of 17. Nicklaus made his name when as a chubby, crew-cut, unphotogenic anti-hero he coolly beat America's sweetheart, Arnold Palmer, in the 1962 U.S. Open at Palmer's home course in Oakmont, Pennsylvania. Nicklaus' powers ebbed and flowed through four phases of a long career before he settled into Senior Tour semi-retirement in the 1990s.

Sam Snead

Slammin' Sammy Snead, a leading player from the 1930s to the 1970s, was the all-time leading tournament winner for the PGA Tour (81, with a total of 135 tournaments worldwide). He was the oldest player to ever win a PGA event, when he took the Greater Greensboro Open in 1965 a few months shy of 53. His last game was a loss in the par-three tournament at the 1992 Masters at age 80. In his lifetime, he won every major competition but one: the U.S. Open. "I'm going to go down in the history books not so much for the 135 tournaments I've won—including the Masters three times, the PGA National three times, and the British Open once—but for the one tournament I never won," Snead philosophized to an interviewer. "I'll tell you a little secret though. I think the fact that I never won that kind of endears me to golf fans. Some anyway. They'd come out and root for me, bless 'em, and my impossible dream in a way became their's too."

Eldrick "Tiger" Woods

Credited with bolstering youth and minority interest in the sport he began playing as a toddler, Woods turned pro shortly after winning an unheard-of third consecutive U.S. Amateur championship. The 1996 PGA Rookie of the Year, Woods won three of the first nine tournaments he entered as a pro and roared past the $1 million mark in winnings in 19 fewer events than the old record. In 1997, he became a history making and record smashing Masters champion.

Greg "Great White Shark" Norman

Despite his lofty earnings and "expensive toys," Greg Norman will forever be remembered more for the tournament he lost than for those he won. Not one to excel during the early stages of the Masters, the morning of April 14, 1996, nevertheless found his name at the top of the leader board with a six-stroke lead going into the final round. That fatal and fateful Sunday, Norman found himself:

to the left at the eighth after a badly pulled second shot; short at the ninth, his approach running back down the hill; left at the 10th, where he compounded his error by half-thinning his chip; above the hole at the 11th, with three putts the result; short and wet at the 12th, championship golf's most treacherous short hole; arguing with his caddie as they debated whether to go for the 13th green in two; left, short and wet again at the 16th after his worst shot of the day; Norman finished the day in second place, shooting a 78, five shots behind winner Nick Faldo.

Other famous names

Nancy Lopez, Byron Nelson, Calvin Peete (first major black golfer), Gary Player, Betsy Rawls, Lee Trevino, Tom Watson, Kathy Whitworth (85 career wins, first female golfer to win $1 million), Mickey Wright, Michael Jordan, Bob Hope, Bing Crosby, Johny Carson, Ike Eisenhower, Bill Clinton, Kramer.

The Rules of Golf

- Although different clubs and associations may articulate them in various ways and assign official-looking numbers to them, the Rules of Golf are universal. Changing them is against the Rules.

General Rules

- You may carry only fourteen **clubs**.

- Play the holes of a golf course in **sequence**. The ball must go into the hole before you start the next hole.

- You must **tee off** between or behind the tee markers within two club lengths behind them. If your ball accidentally falls off the tee, put it back on—no penalty.

- **Strike the ball** with the head of the club. Don't push, scrape, rake or kick it. And don't hit the ball while it's moving.

- Play the same **ball** from the time you start a hole until you finish it. You must ask your opponent or competitor before replacing a damaged ball. Mark your ball with a pencil in case someone else is using an identical ball.

- Once you have started a golf game, you **must finish** unless you fall ill, an official orders you to stop, or lightning strikes.

• During a round of golf, you can't take **practice shots, test** a green by rolling a ball or scraping the surface, seek **advice** from anyone except your caddie or partner, or offer advice to an opponent or competitor. It's okay however, to ask about rules, hazard locations or the position of the flagstick.

Scoring

• In **match play**, each hole is a separate contest. If you are "three up," for instance, having won three more holes than your opponent, you're the winner even if there are still two holes left. If you and your opponent each win nine holes, the resulting tie is called "all square." If your opponent asks how many strokes you have taken on a hole, the Rules require that you tell the truth.

• In **stroke play**, the competitor with the lowest total number of strokes wins.

Order of Play

• Whoever had the lowest score on the last hole gets the **"honor"** of playing first on the next hole. After the tee-off, the person whose ball is farthest from the hole plays first.

• In **match play**, if you play out of turn you can be required to play the shot again. If you play a ball that is not yours, you lose the hole unless the wrong ball was played in a hazard. You must then play the right ball. In **stroke play**, it doesn't really matter if you play out of turn. But there is a two-stroke penalty if you play a ball that is not yours—except in a hazard, where you must go back and play out the hole with your own ball.

Impediments, Obstructions and Hazards

- **Play the ball** as it lies. You can't press the ground down behind the ball or bend or clear any growing vegetation, and you can't move it to a better spot except in the following circumstances:

- As long as you are not in a hazard, you can remove **loose impediments**—leaves, twigs, branches, worms, insects or other natural objects that are not growing or fixed—as long as it doesn't cause your ball to move. You can also remove **movable obstructions**—artificial or man-made objects such as bottles, tin cans or rakes. Sprinkler heads, shelter houses, cart paths, etc., are immovable obstructions. If the ball moves, replace it; there is no penalty.

- You may drop your ball away from an **immovable obstruction,** such as a sprinkler head, shelter house or cart path, if it interferes with your swing or stance. Find the nearest point that is not closer to the hole where you can play without interference. In this and all other cases that call for dropping the ball, stand erect, hold your arm out straight and drop the ball within one club-length of that point. If the dropped ball rolls into a hazard, out of hazard, more than two club-lengths, nearer the hole, or back into the obstruction or ground under repair, you must drop it again. If the same thing happens again, you must place the ball where it struck the ground on the last drop.

- If your ball or your stance is in **casual water**—a temporary puddle of water caused by rain or overwatering—you can choose between playing the ball as it lies or finding the nearest place not closer to the hole that is away from the water, and drop the ball within one club-length of that place. Can't find your ball in the water? Then drop another ball within one club-length of the place where your ball entered the area. The same rules apply to **ground under repair**—any damaged area that has been marked as such by course officials—or burrowing animal holes. There is no penalty.

- **Water hazard** boundaries are identified by yellow or red stakes or lines. If your ball lands in a water hazard, you can choose between playing it as it lies (if you can find it) or adding a penalty stroke and dropping and playing another ball either from where you last played or from as far as you wish behind the water hazard so that there is a straight line between the hole, where your ball last crossed the hazard margin and where you drop the ball. In the case of a lateral water hazard, you can also choose to drop a ball within two club-lengths of where your ball last crossed the hazard margin, as long as it is not nearer to the hole.

- If your ball lands in a **hazard**—a sand bunker or a water hazard such as a creek, pond, lake or swamp—and is covered by sand or leaves, you can only remove enough debris so that a portion of the ball is visible. Lifting your

ball to identify it is not allowed in a hazard. (Elsewhere, you can lift your ball to identify it as long as you tell your opponent or competitor first.) In a hazard, do not touch the sand, ground or water with the club before or during your backswing. Nor can you remove loose vegetation or other natural obstructions—but you can move manmade objects such as bottles, rakes or cheesburger wrappers out of the way. If you move a loose impediment within one club length of the ball and the ball moves, add a penalty stroke, replace the ball and play it. If your ball hits another ball and moves it, you must play your ball as it lies, and the owner of the other ball must replace it.

• There is no penalty if you play from off the green and your ball strikes the **flagstick**—unless somebody is holding it.

The Rules of Golf

Other Unfortunate Circumstances

- If your ball is **lost** and can't be found after five minutes of searching, you must add a penalty stroke to your score and play another ball from where you played your last shot. The same rule applies if your ball is ball is **out of bounds**— past the white stakes, fence or wall that marks the boundary of the golf course. If you think your ball may be lost or out of bounds, you may play a **provisional ball** from the place where you played the first ball before you look for the first ball. Then, if you can't find your first ball or find it out of bounds, total the strokes with the first and provisional balls, add a penalty stroke and continue playing with the provisional ball. But if you find your first ball in bounds, continue play with it, pick up the provisional ball and don't count the stroke(s) you played with it.

- If your ball lands in an **unplayable lie**, such as under (or in) a tree, add a penalty stroke and either go back to where you played the last shot and play a ball from there, drop a ball two club lengths away and play from there, or go back as far as you wish on a straight line, keeping the unplayable lie between you and the hole, and drop and play the ball.

- If you **move your ball**, whether accidentally or intentionally, other than by means of a club stroke, replace it, play it and add a one-stroke penalty. If somebody else moves your ball, you must replace it, but there is no penalty. If a force of nature such as wind or water moves your ball, you must play it as it lies. Once you address the ball, if it moves for any reason, replace it and add a penalty stroke.

- If another ball interferes with your swing or is in your line of putt, you may ask the owner of the ball to **lift the ball**. If your ball is near the hole and might serve as a backstop for another player, you may lift it.

- If your ball is deflected by an **outside agency** such as a tree or a bird, there is no penalty and you can play the ball as it lies. (This is called a "rub of the green.") If your ball hits your opponent or a fellow competitor, his caddie, or his equipment, there is no penalty, and you may play the ball as it lies or replay the shot. But if it hits you, your partner, your caddie, or your equipment, in match play you lose the hole; in stroke play, you are penalized two strokes and you must play your ball as it lies.

- If your ball lands on the **wrong green**, drop it within one club length of the nearest place off the green which is not nearer to the hole you are playing.

- You must put a ball-marker down before **lifting the ball** for any reason. Except on the green, no matter what it may have landed in, you may not clean the ball when lifting it for identification, to determine whether it is damaged or to move it out of another player's way. But you may clean your ball when the Rules allow you to lift it for any other reason.

Putting

- When your ball is **on the green**, you can use your hand or a club to brush leaves and other debris out of your line of putt, but you cannot use your cap or a towel. On the putting green, there is no penalty if the ball moves while you are clearing away a loose impediment, but you must replace it. You can repair old ball marks or hole plugs in your path but not spike or heel marks. When picking a ball up from the green to clean or move it out of another player's line of putt, mark its position with a ball marker or small coin. You cannot move another player's marker or coin out of your line of putt. If your ball hits another ball that is also on the green, there is a two-stroke penalty in stroke play but no penalty in match play.

• Do not putt with the **flagstick** in the hole. Take the flagstick out or ask another player to remove it when you play your ball. If your putt hits the flagstick in the hole, in match play you lose the hole. In stroke play, there's a two-stroke penalty.